Take A Beach Walk

By Jane Kirkland
Edited by
Rob Kirkland
Dorothy Burke
Melanie Palaisa

Are You Ready to Discover...

You're about to set out on a beach adventure! Not only will you make discoveries and see things you haven't noticed before, you'll learn more about the plants and animals you can find at the beach. You're also going to help complete this unfinished book by having your own adventures.

I've had lots of beach adventures but one of my favorites happened to me when I was 11 years old. It was an amazing adventure that happened by accident when I was staying with my grandparents in Shipbottom, New Jersey. It was cool to have grandparents that lived at the shore. At one end of their street was the Atlantic Ocean and a beautiful, long white beach. At the other end of the street was the bay where the waters were calm. My brother and I were in the bay where the water was only waist high when my adventure happened.

Just playing around, my brother pushed me and I fell under the water. I came up covered in seaweed. As I pulled the seaweed off I saw something glimmer and move in it. I looked closely and it was a seahorse! I was so excited I could hardly breathe! We put the seahorse and seaweed in a bucket of water.

We watched the seahorse swim around for awhile, then took the bucket home to show my parents. We kept the seahorse in the bucket overnight. The next morning it was dead. I was heartbroken. Later my dad tried to make me feel better and he made the seahorse into a necklace for me.

I loved that seahorse necklace and kept it for years before giving it to one of my nieces. But I would rather the seahorse had lived. I wish now that someone had known enough to warn me that the seahorse would die if I didn't return it to its habitat right away.

I will remember my seahorse adventure for the rest of my life.

A Day to Remember

I hope you have exciting adventures on your beach walk. I hope you discover birds, plants, insects, crabs, clams, shells, sand dollars, and so much more! And if you should find a live seahorse, please return it to its habitat quickly.

I accidently caught a sea horse just like this one! It was such a surprise to me—what luck—what magic!

...Nature at the Beach?

The book will teach you how to find, observe, and identify plants and animals along sandy shorelines of North American Atlantic, Pacific, and Gulf coasts. There are hundreds of plants and animals you can find and observe on and near the beach. You'll learn about many of them in this book. You'll also learn how an ordinary day at the beach can turn into an exciting nature discovery!

There are three sections to this book: *Get Ready*, *Get Set*, and *Go*. Here in the *Get Ready* section I'll show you how a beach can be divided into different zones. I'll also help you to prepare for your walk. In the *Get Set* section you'll learn about some very special beach residents. The Go section will show you which plants and animals to look for in the different areas of the beach. It also contains a page for you to take field notes, a page to record your observations, and photos to help you identify the plants and animals you find. Throughout this book you'll find artwork by kids and fun and interesting sidebars.

Take a friend or family member with you on your nature walk. It's so much more fun to make new discoveries when you have someone to share them with. My friends Emily and Anders Beckman are both friends and family—they're sister and brother!

Once you know where to look and what to look for you'll see just how exciting a beach walk can be! There's so much nature at the beach that soon you'll wonder how you didn't notice it before! You can read this book in any order you wish. Just remember that this book isn't finished until you go outside to explore! Are you ready to discover nature at the beach?

Be Prepared

Dress properly. Wear the right amount of sunscreen to protect your skin, insect repellent if necessary, a hat to shade your eyes, and the right clothes for the temperature. Sunglasses are a good idea but you'll have to remove them to see the colors of plants and animals to identify them. Wearing sandals to protect your feet is a good idea, too, because if you're looking up at birds you aren't looking to see where you're walking—ouch!

Take this book. This book will help you identify the species you find.

Leave only footprints. Don't litter on the beach—don't leave your gum, water bottles—anything.

Where are the Sharks?

You won't find many fish, dolphins or whales in this book because this book focuses on the things you find along the beach—not deep in the water. But if you're lucky, you can see them from the beach.

New Words?

Habitat (HAb-i-tat):

Where one lives. An animal's habitat is the part of the environment in which it lives.

Species (SPEE-shees):

A certain kind, variety, or type of living creature.

Maritime (MAR-eh-time):

Of, relating to, or bordering on the sea. A maritime forest is a forest near or on the ocean.

What Are Tides?

Tides are changes in the surface level of oceans, bays, and other large bodies of water caused by the gravitational pull of the moon and the sun. There are two high tides and two low tides every day.

A sandy beach contains different zones, each a different *habitat.* Each habitat supports many **species** of plants and animals. In the painting below, the zones are labeled. On the right page you can see the littoral **(LIT-er-uhl)** zone. It's the area of the beach between the low tide line and the high tide line. Moving away from the water, next is the berm—the sandy ridge of the high tide line. The upper beach is often flat and the dry sand there makes it a great place to play volleyball. No plants can grow here because they can't anchor their roots in the constantly moving sand.

Then the dunes begin—if there are dunes on your beach. Dunes are sand hills formed by the wind. The dunes are where the plants grow along the beach. The dunes are divided into several zones, beginning with the primary dune or dunes, those closest to the water. The secondary dune or dunes are smaller hills behind the primary dune where grasses and wildflowers grow. Moving further away from the water is the shrub zone where dense vegetation begins. And finally, the maritime forest.

When you're exploring the beach it helps to know which zones to explore and what plants and animals to look for in those zones. So look up and down your beach to see if you can identify the different zones. This will help you later when you're exploring for plants and animals.

Maritime Forest   Shrub Zone (Thicket)   Secondary Dune (Interdune)

...Do You Want to Explore?

Most people look at a sandy beach and see, well, just sand! You're going to learn how to see much more than that! But have you ever wondered where sand comes from and what it is? Sand is small grains of different materials. Most sand contains large amounts of quartz and feldspar, two minerals found in mountains and cliffs. How do the minerals become sand? They are worn down over time by water and wind and get washed into rivers and streams, finally ending up in the ocean. Sand can also contain smashed up shells and coral, lava rock, decayed

*The quartz grains in sand are easy to see—they are **translucent**.*

marine plants, fossils, and other rocks. The materials found in the sand are what give sand its color, which is different in different areas of North America. There are white, gray, and beige beaches, all made of different materials.

Sand moves around constantly. Waves, tides, winds and storms move it around, sometimes washing it ashore and other times taking it out to sea.

New Word?

Translucent (tranz-LOOSE-ent):

*Clear enough to allow light to pass through but not so clear you can see through it. If something is clear enough to see through, it is **transparent**.*

Know Where You Can Go

On most beaches, walking on the sand dunes is not permitted. On some beaches, at certain times of year, areas are roped off to protect nesting birds. Wet rocks can be slippery and dangerous. Read the signs that are posted on the beach and respect what they say. If they say "Stay off", then stay off.

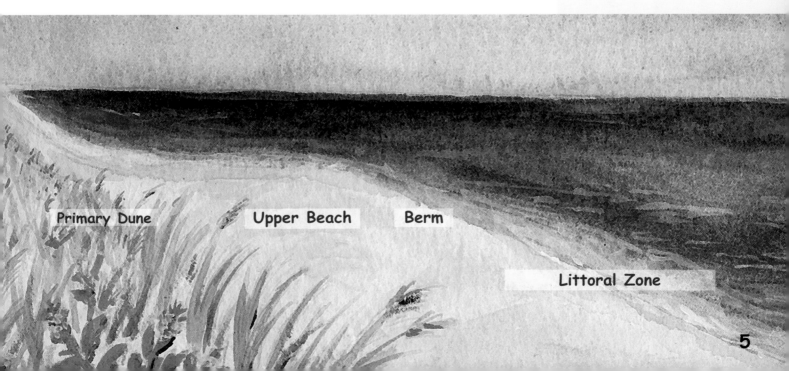

Primary Dune   Upper Beach   Berm

Littoral Zone

New Word?

Plumage (PLEW-mij)

The feathers that cover a bird's body.

Beach Poetry

Across the narrow beach we flit,
One little sandpiper and I,
And fast I gather, bit by bit,
The scattered driftwood bleached and dry.
The wild waves reach their hands for it,
The wild wind raves, the tide runs high,
As up and down the beach we flit,—
One little sandpiper and I.

—From The Sandpiper by Celia Thaxter

Where are the Seagulls?

Here's a riddle for you. Why can't you find seagulls in a field guide to birds? Because there is no such species! People call gulls "seagulls" but there's no family or species of birds named "seagull". Therefore, you won't find a seagull in a field guide to birds.

Sandpipers by Brielle Jeffries, age 9, Beach Haven, NJ.

You'll see a lot of birds at the beach. Three of the most common groups are the gulls, terns, and sandpipers. But do you know the difference between them? It's easy—let me show you how—starting with gulls.

Gulls are the noisiest and most widespread birds at the beach. They have webbed feet and hooked bills. They also have different plumage in different seasons. Gulls can be seen flying over the water, over the land, hanging out in parking lots and back yards, on piers and docks, and, well, just about everywhere! Gulls eat almost anything—anywhere—and at any time. They can be very aggressive and will even steal bait from a fisherman or lunch from a kid! It's not a good idea to feed gulls—they know perfectly well how to find their own food.

Laughing gulls are so good at finding food that they sometimes sit on Pelicans waiting for the right opportunity to steal food from the Pelican's pouch! This Laughing Gull is in winter plumage.

The Ring-billed, Herring, and Laughing gulls are wide spread. The Laughing Gull is found on the Atlantic and Gulf coasts the other two are also found on the Pacific Coast. They are shown here in breeding plumage. Whenever you observe gulls, notice the color of their bills and legs. These keys will help you to identify them.

The Herring Gull (top right) has a yellow bill with a red spot and pale pink legs. The Ring-billed Gull, top left, has a yellow bill with a black ring, and yellow legs and eyes. The Laughing Gull has a black head and a deep red bill. Its call sounds like a loud laugh—ha ha ha ha haaaah!.

...To Tell These Birds Apart

Many people mistake terns for gulls. Here are five clues to help you tell the difference: clue #1: Terns are generally smaller than gulls. Clue #2: Terns have pointed bills but gulls have hooked bills. Clue #3: Terns fly over the water looking for food. Gulls usually eat while on the land. Clue #4: Terns won't beg for food like gulls do. Terns eat fish and they like to catch their own. And clue #5, Terns dive into the water to catch their food, gulls don't dive. With these clues, I bet you can tell a tern from a gull starting today!

Sandpipers are another large group of shorebirds. They have straight, thin beaks which they use to probe mud and sand to find food. Sandpipers are fun to watch as they scatter about the mud and water's edge looking for food. They often fly in formation—all at once, in large groups, zigzagging across the sky.

Look around on the beach for these three families of birds. Because their plumage changes with the seasons, it can sometimes be difficult to identify a particular species of gull, tern, or sandpiper. That doesn't matter—you don't have to be an expert. Believe me, if you can tell a gull from a tern or a sandpiper, you know more than most people. Congratulations!

You can usually tell a tern from a gull in flight. Terns tend to fly over the water looking for food with their beaks pointed down toward the water like this Forster's Tern.

Sanderlings are small sandpipers that run along the edge of the waves looking for food. In the spring when they travel north to their Arctic nesting grounds, their plumage is reddish. On their trip south in the fall, they are gray like those shown above.

Cheat Sheet

The behavior of a bird—what it is doing when you see it—is a clue to identifying the family and species. Here are the three behavior clues to figuring out if a bird is a member of the gull, tern, or sandpiper family:

1. Hooked bill, noisily begging for food— it's a gull!

2. Flying or hovering over water, beak pointing down at the water and diving for food—it's a tern.

3. Running on the beach, along the edge of the water, in and out as if it doesn't want to get its feet wet—it's a sandpiper.

Most Famous Gull?

Perhaps the most famous gull in the world is Jonathan Livingston Seagull. He's a fictional character in a book by the same name. The book is about a gull that sets out to be more than "just a seagull". Jonathan Livingston Seagull is written by Richard Bach.

Clam by Kaylee Autumn Williams, age 8, Little Egg Harbor, NJ.

New Words?

**Exoskeleton
(EX-oh-skel-uh-tun)**

An animal's shell. "Exo" means outside so an exoskeleton is a skeleton on the outside of the body. Insects have exoskeletons. "Endo" means inside. Humans have endoskeletons.

**Adaptations
(a-dap-TAY-shens)**

Changes that a species makes to help it survive when its environment, food source, or world changes. Adaptations take place over many generations.

**Camouflage
(KAM-uh-flaj)**

Coloring or patterns that help and animal hide or blend in with its environment.

*Ever listen to a shell?
Could you hear the ocean well?
I call the sound the Mollusk Mash.
I think it could be a huge smash!*

Do you know all seashells are skeletons? Seashells are the skeletons of mollusks. Because they grow on the outside of the animal, they are called *exoskeletons*. Mollusk shells help protect mollusks from predators.

Clams are mollusks. So are oysters, mussels, conches, snails, squids, and octopuses. Squids and Octopuses don't have external shells, but most of the other mollusks do.

Shells come in lots of different shapes and sizes. Shells are examples of *adaptations*. For example, the shapes of some snail shells help to keep them from sinking in the mud. Some shells are shaped in a way that attracts algae to grow on them, which helps them to be *camouflaged*. Other shells are heavy and thick so they don't wash away in the waves and tides.

If you visit a beach that has tons of shells (such as Sanibel Island, Florida) think about all the mollusks that once lived in all of those shells. That's a lot of mollusks! Where did all those mollusks go? I don't know where every one of them went but an awful lot ended up in the bellies of predators that have the ability to extract the mollusk from its shell or crack the shell open.

Mollusks may not be warm and fuzzy animals but you gotta just love them. After all, they gave us all those shells on the beach. And of course, they also taste good!

So when you're collecting and identifying shells, be sure to thank the mollusks. Oh, and be sure to look inside your shell to see if any mollusks are still there.

Conches (top), clams (bottom left) and snails (bottom right) are all mollusks.

...Crusty, Crabby Crustaceans

Other creatures have shells, too, but they aren't the kinds of seashells we like to collect. Crustaceans (kruh-STAY-shuns) have shells. They are a group of animals related to insects. Crabs, lobsters, and shrimp are all crustaceans. But you won't find too many lobsters and shrimp on the beach—they live in deep water. You can find crabs, though, because lots of crabs live near or on the beach.

I think crabs are one of the coolest creatures on the beach. First of all, they can walk forward and backward. Because of the way their legs are jointed, they can run the fastest when they run sideways! It's pretty funny to watch a crab—with its five sets of legs running sideways. Their exoskeletons protect them from the hot sun and from predators. They can also burrow into the sand. Some crabs live in water, they can swim, and they have gills! Other crabs live on land. Some crabs have eyes on tops of stems that stick out above their body. To me, crabs are the king of the beach!

Ghost Crabs are active on the sand of east and Gulf coast beaches at night. They get their name because they blend in so well with the sand that they seem to suddenly appear and then suddenly disappear.

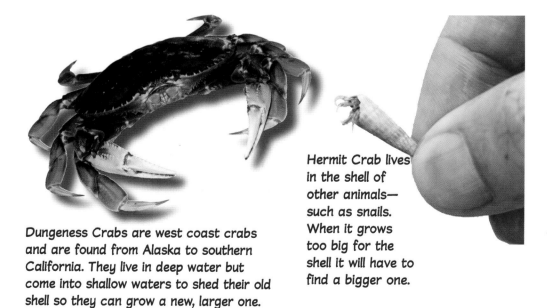

Dungeness Crabs are west coast crabs and are found from Alaska to southern California. They live in deep water but come into shallow waters to shed their old shell so they can grow a new, larger one.

Hermit Crab lives in the shell of other animals—such as snails. When it grows too big for the shell it will have to find a bigger one.

One Crabby Summer

One summer my husband Reds and I took my 12-year old sister and 9-year old brother out in a small boat to catch crabs. We rowed out into the bay where we caught about 36 crabs. Our crab basket was nearly full. Then brother tripped while hauling in a crab and knocked over the crab basket! Suddenly, all the crabs were loose in the boat—pinching, running sideways, and clawing at us. We were all screaming and jumping around. We all moved to one end of the rowboat and the rowboat nearly tipped over. My brother and sister were so afraid they jumped overboard! Then, afraid that the crabs would jump overboard and come after them, they swam all way to the beach to get out of the water! Meanwhile my husband collected all the crabs in the boat and put them back in the basket. We still laugh about that crabby adventure!

Oh, you might know my sister. Her name is Jane and she is the author of this book. Our crab adventure took place in the same bay where Jane found her seahorse and where I live today. Who knew?

*Joyce McKinney,
Shipbottom, New Jersey*

Linda Rowan—a BBFF

Birdwatchers are a Bird's Best Friend Forever (BBFF). It is because of them that we know when bird populations are rising or declining. A birdwatcher is a sort of bird scientist but at the same time, a regular person like you and me and my friend Linda Rowan, who writes:

It was birdwatchers who first reported that the shorebird numbers were declining during the Horseshoe Crab spawning on Delaware Bay. Because of their observations, formal studies were launched and conservation efforts have started to try to protect the Horseshoe Crabs and help the Red Knots that feed on the eggs.

Birdwatchers keep lists of the birds they see. They participate in special bird counts such as the Christmas Bird Count and Migratory Bird Count. And they report their sightings to organizations like National Audubon and The Cornell Laboratory of Ornithology. Because of these "citizen scientists", we know more about birds and bird populations than ever before.

Birdwatching is one of the fastest growing hobbies in the U.S. Learn more about birdwatching at:

www.audubon.org

www.birds.cornell.edu

When is a crab not a crab? When it's a *Horseshoe Crab*—an animal that's not even a crustacean! Horseshoe Crabs can be found from the Gulf of Maine to the Gulf of Mexico. Every May they come ashore to lay their eggs (spawn) and save the lives of hundreds of thousands of shorebirds. And the largest concentration of spawning Horseshoe Crabs on the Atlantic coast happens in the Delaware Bay, not far from my home. For several years, my husband Rob and I have photographed the spawning. It's an incredible site!

Each female crab lays up to 90,000 eggs in several nests. So many crabs come ashore at the same time that they overturn each other's nests while digging their own. They also get overturned themselves and when this happens, they could die if they are too exhausted to turn back over. We turn them over when we can.

So how do the Horseshoe crabs save the shorebirds? Their eggs provide vital food for shorebirds at a critical time in their migration north.

Crabs everywhere (top): it was difficult to walk on the beach for all the crabs. Birds everywhere (middle): these were some hungry birds—just waiting for the crabs to come ashore. Eggs everywhere (bottom): I never saw so many eggs! These were smaller than peas and piled as much as 1" high in this tidal pool, washed there by the waves.

...Most Prehistoric Character

When the Horseshoe Crabs spawn in May, the shorebirds arrive to gorge on their eggs. Some birds double their body weight on eggs before continuing north to their breeding grounds. The eggs they eat are located too close to the surface to survive even if the birds didn't eat them. So the gorging doesn't affect the population of the Horseshoe Crabs. But something else does—harvesting. Commercial fishermen use horseshoe crabs for fish bait. We've harvested so many Horseshoe Crabs that their population numbers are down. As a result, so are the numbers of shorebirds, especially the Red Knots, who depend on the Horseshoe Crabs for survival.

Over twenty species of shorebirds rely on the Horseshoe Crab spawning. And 95% of those birds are one of only four species: the Red Knot (above), Ruddy Turnstone (below), Sanderlings, and Semipalmated Sandpipers.

The Red Knots are in big trouble. They have one of the longest and hardest migrations of any bird. They arrive at the Delaware Bay in May after a 5000-mile flight and they are very, very hungry. After their stopover they still

have another 4500 miles to their nesting grounds in the arctic. Without plenty of crab eggs to eat, they won't make it or, if they do, they won't be strong enough to raise their young. But each year there are fewer and fewer crabs laying eggs. As a result Red Knots are in danger of becoming extinct in a few years. To learn more about Horseshoe Crabs, Red Knots and this problem, visit: **www.horseshoecrab.org.**

Crab Chix Chats

My friends Trish Schuster and Beth Huch are Horseshoe Crab experts. They call themselves the "Crab Chix" and they teach others about Horseshoe Crabs.

Do you know that Horseshoe Crabs have probably saved your life with their special blue blood? How? Well, those vaccines you had to have to go to school are tested with Horseshoe Crab blood.

Do you know that Horseshoe Crabs have ten eyes? And that, despite all those claws, they are harmless to pick up. Their tail, or telson, is not a weapon but a lever used to right themselves! And you should never pick up a Horseshoe Crab by its tail or you can harm it. These are just a few of the things I've learned from Trish and Beth. I just love chatting with the Crab Chix!

A horseshoe might be dull.
A horseshoe might be drab.
But a horseshoe is—well,
Definitely not a crab!

The Take A Walk® Poem

Today I saw a big black bird
fly high up in the sky.
I walked into a garden where I
found a butterfly.
A squirrel was busy working as
he jumped from tree to tree.
Was I dreaming when I saw a
cloud smiling back at me?

I felt the warm sun on my
face, I heard a robin sing.
I smelled the sweetness in the
air—I noticed everything!
Where were these things
before today? How could I
not have known?
Is this because I'm older now?
Is this because I've grown?

So much did I encounter that I
can't wait to learn more.
About the things that I can
find just outside my door.
But the best part of my walk
today was my discovery—
That every time I take a walk,
I learn more about me!

By Jane Kirkland
With contributions by
Emily Heckman, age 9

Horseshoe Crab by Alex Kim,
age 10, Malvern, PA.

A naturalist is someone who studies nature. Can you guess what a beach naturalist does? He is someone who studies, explores, observes, and cares for nature at the beach.

A naturalist can read the signs around him. Not just the signs like those pictured here, but signs of nature. For example, he looks for animal tracks so he knows which animals are nearby. He looks for changes in the weather so he knows when it's time to head back to shelter. He listens for birds and other animals. He smells the air for signs of fragrant plants or stinky animals.

Not only does a naturalist read the signs of nature, he writes about nature and draws pictures in his field notes. Field notes can help you to remember your beach walk. You can write about the weather, the things you found, and the things you observed during your beach walk. You can take notes while you're exploring the beach or after you get back home. You'll also find another place to take notes and draw pictures on page 21.

If you take field notes every time you take a beach walk you can compare your notes. You'll see different plants and animals in different seasons at the beach.

Today you are a beach naturalist. The beach is your field and all of the nature in it is yours to explore, observe, and study. Good on ya!

Salty sea spray takes its toll on everything at the beach—even the signs. Whenever you're at the beach pay attention to the signs so you know where danger lurks and where you are permitted to walk, swim, and take your dog.

...Write Your Field Notes

Your Field Notes Page

Use this form or blank paper for your Field Notes. If you need more forms you can download them for free at our website. Your field notes should include today's date and your location (the name of the beach you are exploring). You can even put what zone of the beach you're exploring or some other landmark to explain where you are on the beach (such as a street or building name). Fill in the time of day you are exploring. Write about today's weather: the temperature, what the sky looks like, and so forth. You can also use this form to list the plants and animals you see. Write what you can now, and then add more during and after your walk.

Hermit Crab by Joseph Letinski, age 10, Barnegat NJ.

Anemone by Gianna Letinski, age 10, Barnegat NJ.

Need more room to draw or write? Use blank paper or download free forms at www.takeawalk.com.

A Favorite

This is one of my favorite books about nature on the beaches of our southeastern coast. It is beautifully illustrated by the author. It looks and feels like his personal journal of nature at the beach.

Tideland Treasure

Written by Todd Ballantine. Published by University of South Carolina Press.

Hermit Crab by Brian Santos, age 10, Toms River, NJ.

Sea floor by Kevin Santos, age 8, Toms River, NJ.

Snake by Mary Jane Costello, age 11, Little Egg Harbor, NJ.

The littoral zone has several names. It is also called the intertidal (in-ter-tide-uhl) zone and the splash zone. It's a harsh place for plants and animals to live. When the tide is high, the sand is under water. When the tide is low, the sand and the plants and animals found there are exposed to the sun, predators, and salt spray. Nights can be cold and days can be very hot.

Plants and animals that live here have adapted to survive extreme conditions. Mole Crabs have smooth and rounded shapes to help them burrow quickly to avoid the crashing waves and predators. Some seaweed can get completely dried out in the sun during low tide, then drowned during high tide and still survive. Some birds have long beaks to probe the sand for food and others have beaks that can break open clams and other prey hiding in shells. Around the beach, it's adapt or die!

I think the Mole Crab looks like Rhinoceros! These little guys are always on the move. In the spring tides carry them to the beach where they live until the fall. In winter, tides carry them out to sand bars. They aren't true crabs but they are crustaceans.

At first glance you might not see much in the littoral zone. But once you know where to look and what to look for, you can find lots of treasures.

The littoral zone is where you'll find shells. The best time to go shell hunting is early in the morning—at low tide if possible.

...Lively Littoral Zone

Have you ever noticed a wavy band of junky stuff along the beach? That is called the *strandline*. It is the line of things washed ashore by the high tide. Here you'll find seaweed, different creatures of the sea and sand, driftwood, seeds such as acorns and sweetgum balls that fall off trees and wash into the ocean from streams. You'll also find flotsam and jetsam. Flotsam are man-made things that accidentally end up in the sea (such as the remains of a shipwreck). Jetsam are things that people throw into the sea (like notes in a bottle). Winds, tides and waves carry these things to shore.

The entire littoral zone is exciting to explore. Besides the beach and the strandline, look here for more:

- **The water's edge**. Dig to find Mole Crabs and other burrowing animals. You don't need a shovel—use your hands.

- **The tidal pools**. Look for sand dollars, sea stars, sea jellies, and more!

And while you're exploring, don't forget to look up at the sky for birds!

The strandline contains clues to plants and animals that live just offshore. Insects and other creatures found here are a source of food to other animals.

My friend Liz Armidon likes to explore tidal pools. Tidal pools are the pools of water that remain on the sand or among the rocks at low tide.

This is called a "mermaid's purse". It's an egg case from a Skate (a kind of ray fish related to sharks and rays). Look for these washed up in the strandline.

American Littoral Society

Jim Peck is a naturalist and the Education Coordinator for the American Littoral Society. They are an organization dedicated to teaching people about our coasts and showing them how to care for it. Jim taught me to notice the transitions between beach zones—sometimes it's so easy to recognize the different zones. He reminded me that wind, tides, and storms are always moving sand from the sand bars in the water to the beach and the dunes. He calls this movement of sand a "wonderful dance with nature". Jim and the other members of the American Littoral Society know so much about coastal areas! I admire their knowledge and their work to educate others. I want to make them my new BFFs! Learn more at:

www.littoralsociety.org

Man Against Nature

Humans like our beaches clean, flat, and wide. Every day man and his machines run along beaches clearing the strandlines away. Storms create beach erosion and as soon as a big storm is over, humans are rebuilding the beaches. Don't you think it's interesting how humans often put our own needs above nature's plan? The beach isn't the only example of man against nature. Can you think of other examples?

Keep Off the Dunes—Why?

Sand dunes can be really fun to slide down, but the roots of the dune grass are very shallow and even a few footsteps can destroy the vegetation. The "toe" of the sand dune (the area at the bottom of the dune) is very sensitive to trampling and beach blankets. Before you throw down your beach blanket or towel, make sure there is no vegetation. And never climb the dunes or touch the dunes for any reason.

Storms, heavy winds and heavy waves carry sand away. Smaller waves deposit sand on the beach and mild winds blow it up to the dunes. Dunes need plants to trap wind-blown sand. The sand hits the plants and falls to the ground, then the growing roots bind the new sand. The dune grows as the sand accumulates after being trapped and stabilized by the grass. Sometimes you might hear about a Scout group going to the beach to plant dune grass for a project—now you know why!

Mary Judge
Barnegat Bay Estuary

Many people think that the dunes are just big piles of sand. But dunes are important habitats. They also help us during storms—keeping high waves from reaching inland. They protect our houses and habitats from being destroyed by the force of the storm's waves. Dunes are much more than just big piles of sand!

Really cool things can wash up onto the beach and even up to the dunes. Check out these whale bones (above) and driftwood (below). That's Rob (my husband) on the back side of the dune.

You can find quite a few animals and plants in the dunes. You might see rabbits, raccoons, mice, birds, lizards, snakes, or insects. Look for their tracks in the fine sand.

Notice how different plants grow on different areas of the dunes. On the seaward side—the side facing the ocean—salt, wind and shifting sands make it difficult for plants to survive. Plants there grow low to the ground and tolerate the hot sun. Look for signs of plant adaptations such as tiny hairs which can catch salt in the air before it touches the plant or thick leaves which help plants to retain moisture. The tops of the dunes are very dry and get lots of wind. Only plants that can tolerate dryness can grow there. The back side of the dunes is protected from wind and sea spray—a much more plant-friendly environment.

As you get further from the ocean the ground becomes more stable and plants are less exposed to wind and salt spray, so you see different and more diverse communities of plants and animals.

...Dynamic Dunes, Dude!

The grains of sand on the dunes are very fine. So fine that everything that touches it leaves a trail in the sand. Even something as light as a blade of grass leaves a trail in dune sand.

How are dunes formed? By sand blowing around in the wind. Some dunes are so large you might think it would take huge windstorm to make them. But dunes build over time and the sand itself helps the wind to move

The Yellow-rumped Warbler is a common resident of the dune shrub and forest areas. Their nickname among birdwatchers is "Butter Butt".

sand around. Here's how: when wind lifts the sand and drops it back down the grains bounce off the sand on the ground. When the sand grains bounce, they make other sand grains pop up and those get caught in the wind, too. Sand keeps piling up and dunes get higher. After awhile the piles of sand are so steep that they fall down in an avalanche. Sometimes the avalanches are big, sometimes they are small.

All this movement of sand is such an interesting thing to watch—you should try it sometime. Do what I do—just sit down next to the dune on a breezy day and watch the sand blowing, dropping, crashing, popping, piling, and falling around. Listen to the grasses

Sea Oats help build sand dunes by helping to stabilize the sand. They are so important to dune structure that it's illegal to cut them down.

and the sand blowing in the wind. From high up on the dunes where paths lead to the ocean, you can get a good view of the water. Maybe you'll see a dolphin or two!

Beach Pollution

Can you guess what are the major causes of beach pollution? Here are a few:

Land-based sewer systems. Older sewer systems can flush our toilet water directly into the rivers and ocean after a big rain storm.

Litter. Do I really need to explain what litter is?

Oil spills. Every time we have an oil spill from a ship carrying oil, animals get covered with black, yucky, sticky, gooey, disgusting oil. As long as we continue to need and use as much oil as we do in this country, we'll continue to have to live with oil spills.

Storm drain run-off. Although rain water is pretty clean when it falls from the sky, a heavy rain can cause flooding, which can then wash every bit of trash that was lying around into the rivers and the ocean.

Developments built on the beach. Construction projects always make a mess. They break up the ground so that even a little bit of rain will carry away all sorts of mud and debris. After a development is finished, more people come to the beach where they litter and take their boats out in the water and dump their sewage.

Will the circle ever be broken?

Animal Kingdoms

Biologists classify living creatures according to their physical characteristics. Those classifications are: kingdoms, then phylums (for animals) or divisions (for plants) followed by classes, orders, families, genuses, and species. For example, human beings are:

Kingdom=animalia
Phylum=chordata
class=mammals
order=primates
Genus=homo
Species=sapiens

Crabs are

Kingdom=animalia
Phylum=arthropoda
Class=crustacea
Order=decopada

Check it out—crabs are arthropods. And so are spiders and insects! Relatives! Who knew?

Pipefish (see photo opposite page) are:

Kingdom=animalia
Phylum=chordata
Class=actinopterygii
Order=synghathidae

Pipefish have a long snout and look sort of like a straight-bodied seahorse, don't you think? And guess what? Seahorses belong to the synghathidae order, too. And seahorses and some pipefish have prehensile tails—they can grab onto things with their tails— just like monkeys. WOW.

What's an Estuary? An estuary is a body of water where freshwater from a river mixes with saltwater from the ocean. This mixed water is called *brackish* water and it contains less salt than ocean water. Estuaries are very important ecosystems. They support countless species of living things. There are three main reasons for this.

First, the brackish water is more tolerable to young animals. Second, estuaries are partly protected by land so the air and water in them are calmer than on the open ocean. Third, the tides cause the water in estuaries to flow in two directions. During the time between high tide and low tide, when the water levels are going down, the river water flows downstream and out to sea. But when the tide rises, the ocean water level becomes higher than the water level at the mouth of the river, and the water flows upstream, back into the river.

This two-way flow of water provides a very rich environment for animals. First the water carries nutrients downstream. Then it carries them back upstream. The animals can just sit in one nice hiding place and wait for the flowing water to bring food to them. Many animals do just that, including many worms and mollusks and the young of many species of fish.

Estuaries contain many different habitats such as salt marshes, mud flats, rocky shores, and beaches. They have more life per square inch than forests or farmland. Like farmland, they supply us with lots of food. Do you eat anything that comes from an estuary?

This Osprey is bringing a stick to its nest. They like to nest near the water and often nest on man-made platforms such as buoys. They use their talons (claws) to catch fish.

We pulled off the road to take this photo of Fiddler Crabs in an estuary. Male Fiddler crabs have one huge, oversized claw that they wave around to attract females. It didn't work on me (tee-hee).

...Exciting Estuary Ecosystems

Estuary beaches, with their calm waters and gentle winds, are a breeze to explore. Both my seahorse and crab adventures happened to me on an estuary beach. You might not see a seahorse but you will see a lot of animals—and two of the easiest to see are crabs and birds.

Crabs are everywhere in estuaries. Especially along the exposed mud banks along the creeks. There you might see whole cities of Fiddler Crabs sitting at the entrances to their burrows. If they see you, they'll duck inside. If they think you've left, they'll come out again. I guess they don't trust us—we are, after all, predators. Smart crabs!

Birds are everywhere in the estuaries, too. They may be hunting for food—diving, or wading. They may be nesting. They may be singing to establish their territories. See how many different species you can see.

One day Rob and I explored an estuary beach with some friends. We found some cool things on the beach and we used a net to capture some animals in the water. After we photographed them we returned them to their habitat. You can see some of the creatures we found in these photos.

Our estuary treasures from top to bottom: an oyster, a sea star, a Razor Clam, a Pipefish and a Lady Bird Beetle (which some people call a "ladybug").

Please Make Me Pull Over

Mud flats and salt marshes aren't always accessible by foot. But we often have to drive past or through them to get to the beach at the ocean. Roads to the beach often have places where people can pull off and park to fish. Ask your parents if they'll pull off the road so you can look out over the mud flats and salt marshes for birds and crabs.

Where's the Mosquitoes?

You won't find any mosquitoes, flies, or rats in this book—but you can find them at the beach. Let's face it, they are pests. I'd rather focus on the fun creatures. Hope you don't mind. ☺

Which crustacean loves to roam
And borrows shells to make his home?
Try to guess—just take a stab.
Did you guess a hermit crab?

Knock Knock

You can't always tell if there is a live animal in the shell you find at the beach. To be sure that an animal isn't hiding inside, put your shell in a bucket of seawater. Observe it for awhile. If there is an animal inside, and you aren't bothering it in any way, it will eventually feel safe and show part of itself. If you see that happen, return it immediately to where you found it.

Small Field Guides

Here are some of my favorite small, pocket-size field guides for the beach:

Stokes Beginner's Guide to Shorebirds.

By Donald Stokes and Lillian Stokes. Published by Little, Brown & Company.

Peterson First Guide to Seashores.

By John C. Kricher, Gordon Morrison, and Roger Tory Peterson. Published by Houghton Mifflin.

Here's an example of how to create a Nature ID Page. The facing page is a blank form for you to write down details about a plant or animal you see on your beach walk. You can draw it or take a photo of it and paste it on your form page. If it's a species you don't recognize, your notes will help you to identify the species when you research it in a field guide, at the library, or on the Web.

Date, Time, Weather Conditions: June 3. 8 AM. 70 degrees. Walking on the beach with my mom.

Habitat and location. I saw this animal on the beach in the littoral zone and I thought it was dead. It was on its back.

Size and physical description. The body was about 12" long and it had a hard shell. It was dark brown and it had a lot of legs. It had a long, pointed, scary tail.

Behavior Observation (if it is an animal). At first I though it was dead but then I saw the legs moving really slowly. I turned it over and put it at the edge of the water. Then it moved out into the water.

Additional Notes. I was pretty sure it was a Horseshoe Crab but I wasn't positive until my Mom told me it was.

Species Name. A Horseshoe Crab.

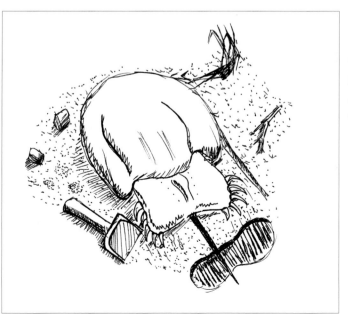

This illustration of a Horseshoe Crab is by Jack Wooldridge, age 11, of Great Meadows, NJ.

...Nature ID Page of Your Own

Date, Time, Weather Conditions:

Habitat and location.

Size and physical description.

Behavior Observation (if it is an animal).

Additional Notes.

Species Name.

(Optional) Make a drawing or paste a photo here:

Need more room to draw or write? Use blank paper or download free forms at www.takeawalk.com.

More Small Field Guides

Here are some more of my favorite small, pocket-size field guides for the beach:

The National Audubon Society (NAS) Pocket Guides are all published by Alfred A. Knopf, Inc. Beach books include:

NAS Pocket Guide to Familiar Seashore Creatures.

NAS Pocket Guide to Familiar Seashells.

Duck by Nicole Maslow, age 12, Darien, IL.

How Can You Tell the Difference?

The picture captions give you clues to identifying these herons and egrets. Clues include their height when standing and the color of their legs and beaks.

Where Can You Find These Birds?

Not every heron and egret on this page is found in every coastal region of North America. Check a bird field guide or a birding website to see their specific ranges.

Egret or Heron?

You can recognize herons and egrets in flight by the way they hold their heads. They fold their long necks back so their heads are close to their bodies. Other long-necked birds (like swans, geese, cranes, and ibises) hold their necks straight, so their heads are way out in front of their bodies when they fly.

**Great Egret
39"
Yellow beak,
black legs.**

**Snowy Egret
24"
Black beak,
yellow feet.**

**Black-crowned
Night Heron
25".**

**Yellow-crowned
Night Heron
24".**

**Great Blue Heron
46"
Yellowish bill,
gray legs.**

**Tricolored Heron
26"
White feathers on
the front of
its throat.**

**Reddish Egret
30"
Red head and neck,
gray legs, pink bill
with dark tip.**

**Little Blue Heron
24"
Blue all over, gray
bill with dark tip,
pale green legs.**

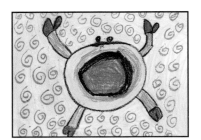

*Crab by Nicole Gangi, age 7,
Brick, NJ.*

*Dolphin by Maegan Farrish, age 9,
Cape May, NJ.*

*Dolphins by Callie Avellino, age 9
Malvern, PA.*

...Check Out These Weird Beaks

Food. When it comes to animals, it's always about the food. Check out these weird beaks. These are some of the coolest beaks on North American coastal birds—each a special adaptation to help birds locate, capture, and in the case of the oystercatcher, open their food. Want to guess what an oystercatcher catches? Hmmm. By the way, food is also the reason that animals migrate. It isn't because the weather is cold; it's because the cold weather kills off the food source. Like I said, when it comes to animals, it's all about the food. My personal favorite here is the Roseate Spoonbill—named for its rosy color and its spoon-shaped bill. No, it doesn't eat spoons, silly!

Where are the Rest of the Birds?

There are a lot more birds that you can see near the coasts—a lot! In fact, we could have done an entire book just on the familiar birds of sea and shore.

Wait a minute! Someone already did. Of course—here's my favorite little field guide that I keep with me when I'm at the beach:

National Audubon Society Pocket Guide **Familiar Birds of Sea and Shore** Alfred A, Knopf, Inc., publisher.

Wood Stork—40". Sweeps beak from side to side in the water to probe for food.

Roseate Spoonbill— 32". Uses spoon-shaped beak to search for food in the water.

White Ibis—25". Also probes the water with its long beak.

Brown Pelican—51". Dives to catch food, using its beak like a net (see sidebar).

Pelican Smellican

North America is also home to American White Pelicans. Brown and White Pelicans are different species with different habitats. The American White Pelican is usually found inland on fresh water. It uses its beak to net food but does not dive like the Brown Pelican, which is a coastal bird.

American Oystercatcher 17.5". Found on the Atlantic and Gulf Coasts. The Black Oystercatcher (all black feathers) is found on the Pacific Coast. They use their specially adapted beaks to break open bivalves.

Black Skimmer 18". The lower half of the beak is longer than the upper half of the beak. It skims the water with its beak open to scoop up food as it flies.

Go! Build Your Own "Best of" List

These are some of my favorite physical and behavioral characteristics of coastal birds. I've given them all "Best of" awards. When you look at birds on the beach, see if you can notice some physical characteristic or behavior that is unusual, unique, or just plain wacky! Then you can build your own "Best of" list.

Best Footwear—the American Coot.

Best Butt Bobber—the Spotted Sandpiper.

Like funk dancers, this bird "pops" constantly but he only pops his butt. When a bird's butt moves up and down, birders say it is "bobbing" its tail. Sandpipers can be difficult to identify because their plumage changes in different seasons. But the behavior of this bobbing butt popper makes the Spotted Sandpiper easy to identify.

The feet of the American Coot look like plant matter. He floats on the water, his feet looking like plants to his prey below, and dives to catch his unsuspecting prey.

Best Marsh Music—the Red-winged Blackbird.

Best in-flight Music—the Belted Kingfisher.

Best Actor in an Injured Role—the Killdeer.

This bird is everywhere in the marsh and easily found by his call. Every spring I look forward to hearing his "kon-ka-reeeee" call.

The Belted Kingfisher has a unique and very loud call that sounds like a rattle. It calls while it flies. If it's nearby, you'll know it.

The Killdeer nests on the ground. If a predator (or human) gets too close to its nest or young, the adult will try to lure it away. It does this by dragging its wing on the ground as if the wing is broken. To a predator, an injured animal is an easy catch.

Go! Focus on Fruits and Flowers

Adaptations help plants survive coastal regions. The Dusty Miller has hairy leaves to protect it from the salt spray. Other plants such as the Ice Plant, Prickly Pear, and Spanish Bayonet help to retain water during the dry season with thick, fleshy leaves. Here are some plants you can see along sandy beaches in North America. Not all plants shown here can be seen in all regions.

Sea Rocket

Beach Rose

Morning Glory

Beach Pea

Seaside Goldenrod

Sea Fig

Common Ice Plant

Spanish Bayonet

Prickly Pear

Yellow Sand Verbena

Dusty Miller

Sea Grapes

Bayberry

Coconut Palm Tree

Handle With Care

When you collect shells, please collect them from the beach. Don't take them from the water or pry them from rocks or other things they might be attached to because those shells are living animals.

Whatever you do, don't collect a bunch of shells (especially conches and whelks) and leave them in your hot car. I learned the hard way that shells can be pretty darn stinky! If you find shells on the beach and take them home, ask your parents to put them in boiling water for a few minutes. This will help kill the smell. But of course, you can't put the car in boiling water—so clean the shells first! To keep a wet, shiny look to your shells, ask your parents to help you paint them with clear nail polish.

State Shells

Some states have official shells. Is your state among them?

AL—Junonia
CT—Eastern Oyster
FL—Horse Conch
GA—Knobbed Whelk
NC—Scotch Bonnet
MA—Wrinkle Whelk
MS—Eastern Oyster
NJ—Knobbed Whelk
NY—Bay Scallop
OR—Oregon Triton
RI—Northern Quahog
SC—Lettered Olive
TX—Prickly Whelk
VA—Eastern Oyster

Spiral shaped shells are formed by a class of mollusks called the Gastropods. Here are just a few of them that are among the favorites of shell collectors. Long spiral shells include wormholes. Wormholes are sometimes found individually and other times in large clumps. Round spirals are snail shells. Hermit Crabs (which are crustaceans) will use empty snail shells (which are mollusks) for protection.

Hermit Crab in Snail shell

Snails

Worm Holes

Conches and whelks are popular collector shells because of their size and beauty. Depending on the species some can be 16" long! You can tell a conch from a whelk by its thick outer lip and a rounded notch near the bottom (see arrows).

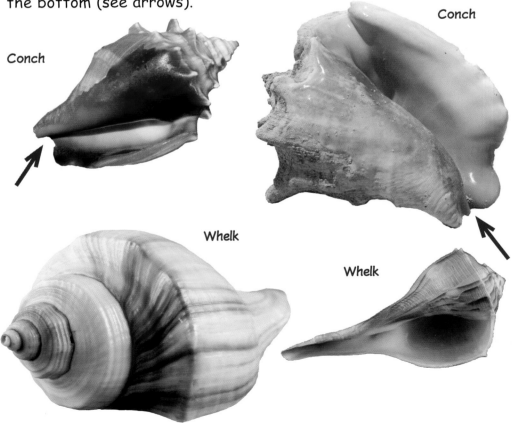

Conch

Conch

Whelk

Whelk

Go! Claim Clam Shaped Shells

Bivalves are mollusks, too. They have a two part shell. "Bi" means two. Bivalves are very popular menu items not only to people but to other animals. This is one example of how being popular is not always a good thing! Just think of all of the animals that eat clams, mussels, oysters, and scallops, just to name a few. Gosh, here I am talking about food again.

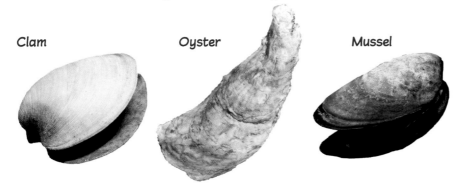

Clam   Oyster   Mussel

People often confuse scallop shells with cockle shells and within each group there are many different kinds. To tell a scallop from other shells, look for the little triangles—some people call them "wings", I like to call them "ears" on each side of the tip (see arrows). This shape makes the shell straight on one side.

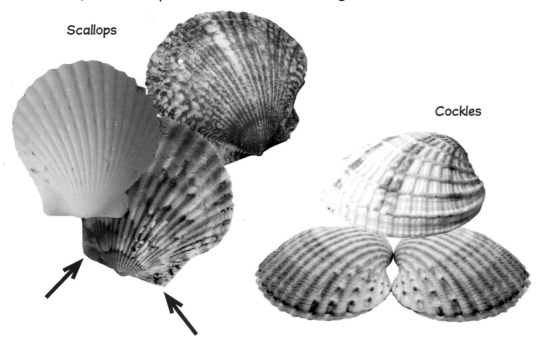

Scallops

Cockles

So Many Shells... So LIttle Time

These two pages represent some of the most common and widespread shells in North America. There are about 700 species of shells in North America. Most shells have ranges. For example, you may only find a given species in the Pacific.

Shells can be difficult to ID. Don't worry too much about identifying them—unless you want to. And if you want to identify them you'll need a good field guide to help you (like the one listed below).

I like to learn about shells the same way I learn about birds. Each season I pick a new group to study and look for in the field. For my beach adventures this year I'm focusing on cockle shells in the summer and sandpipers in the winter. Winter sandpipers are really difficult to identify because their plumage is so different than in the summer. Thank goodness shells don't change color!

Seashell Field Guide

When you need a really good field guide to shells, this is it:

National Audubon Society Field Guide to North American Seashells

Published by Alfred A. Knopf, Inc.

Go! Search for Sea Stars

When is a Fish Not a Fish?

A fish is not a fish when it's a starfish or a jellyfish. Science is always changing. As we learn more about our environment and nature, we discover new species, find new fossils of old ones, and learn how to better categorize plants and animals. Sometimes, we even change their scientific or common names! Both starfish and jellyfish have had a recent common name change. We now call them sea stars and sea jellies.

Sea jellies sometimes wash up onshore, especially after a storm. Some sea jellies can sting. Many animals eat sea jellies. Hmmm. If you or I ate one, we could put it on a peanut butter sandwich and give new meaning to "PB&J".

Another "unfish" is the shellfish. It's a word we use to describe a group of clams, oysters, lobsters and other creatures with shells—none of which are fish. But "shellfish" is easier to say than "a group of mollusks and crustaceans".

Beach scene by Mirish Shah, age 10, Toms River, NJ.

Sea Stars belong to the class of marine animals called Asteroidea. Aster means star. There are lots of species of sea stars and some of them are very colorful. They live on the bottom of the ocean but you can find them in tidal pools (alive) or washed up on the beach (dead). Most sea stars have five arms—but not all. In fact, within a species sea stars can have different numbers of arms.

The mouth of the sea star is very small and located on its underside. It doesn't eat with its mouth. It ejects its stomach from its mouth. Its stomach then surrounds the prey, slowly turning it into a liquid goo. Then the icky goo is absorbed through the stomach lining. If the prey is covered by a shell, the starfish simply spins it around to find the shell opening and then ejects its stomach into the shell of the prey. Yuck! Now I think I can stop talking about food for awhile.

A starfish is not a fish
Or it might look just like this.
Its new name, better by far,
is not starfish but sea star.

Hey, I have a theory. If you find a sea star and then you wish upon a star in the sky while holding a sea star—your wish might come true twice! It's just a theory but it's worth a try, don't you think? And then, if you sang "When You Wish Upon a Star" while wishing on a star in the sky and holding a sea star, it might come true three times! OK, OK, I'll stop. But I'll never stop wishing upon a star—you shouldn't either. I hope you get to see a live sea star while on your beach walk.

This Sea Star has been working out at the gym. How do I know? Just look at his mussel. ☺

Go! Cash in With Sand Dollars

Ka-ching Ka-ching—ahh, the sound of money. To some people, there is no sweeter sound. But to me the bird songs, crashing waves, flags flapping in the wind, and people laughing are all beach sounds sweeter than money. But, do you know that there is money at the beach? Have you ever seen people walking the beach with metal detectors? They're looking for money—and other treasures made of metal. Of course, you can't find dollar bills with a metal detector. But I know where you can find dollars at the beach. Sand dollars, that is.

Sand dollars are neither sand nor dollars. They are the skeleton of a marine animal called an Echinoid (ek-KYE-noid). They are related to the Sea Star and Sea Urchin. Like Sea Stars and Sea Urchins, they are five-sided They're also a major cool find at the beach.

Sand Dollars look very different when they are alive. They're brown and covered with tiny spines that look like hair and that help them to move along the ocean bottom. When they die, they sometimes wash up on the beach. By then, all that's usually left of them is their skeleton.

The best time to find Sand Dollars is while the tide is going out or after a heavy storm when waves wash up those that have died.

Sand Dollars aren't money but finding them is a rich experience. Good luck!

Check out this collection of Sand Dollars laid out on a picnic table. Sand Dollar skeletons have lots of pores (little holes) in them, which look like a five-petal flower in the center. This species, called the Keyhole Sand Dollar, also has 5 large holes that look like slots. There is a sand dollar on the cover of this book. Did you notice?

Fix Your Hair

A beachcomber is someone who searches along beaches or in wharf areas to see what the ocean has washed up or what other people have left behind. People who search the beach with metal detectors are beachcombers. To "comb" means to search thoroughly. When I was little, I thought that a beachcomber was one of those beach cleaning machines that clean up trash and sift the sand. The sand had lines in it after the beach machine ran over it and the sand looked as if it had been combed—like hair. But those machines are called "beach rakes" not "beach combs." Oh well. If you can't find many shells at your beach, maybe the beach rake beat you to it!

Seashell Art

Shells are really beautiful. You can make some very cool art from shells with this book:

Look What I Did With A Shell

By Morteza E. Sohi
Published by Walker Books
for Young Readers.

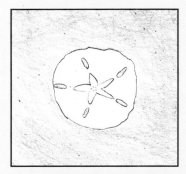

Sand Dollar by Mary-Kate Fogel, age 11, Little Egg Harbor, NJ.

Seahorse Factoids

Seahorses are fishes that can be found around the world Only the male seahorse gets pregnant and the young grow in his brood pouch for weeks. His female partner stays near him dancing with him each day until he gives birth and is ready to accept more eggs

Unfortunately, humans have taken too many seahorses for medicine and aquariums. People's curiosity about seahorses and the destruction of seahorse habitats have put many species of seahorses on endangered lists and unless we do something to help, some could become extinct.

If a seahorse were really a horse I think it would look like this—of course.

Sometimes changes are needed to make our planet a better place to live. And to make those changes we sometimes have to think differently, act differently, or live our lives differently. And even though there are billions of people on our planet, change often begins with a single person. One person can make a difference—for people as well as animals.

Dr. Amanda Vincent is making a difference in the lives of animals. She is the world's leading seahorse biologist. A biologist is a scientist who studies living things—where and how something lives, what it eats, how it reproduces, and how it interacts with other creatures or with its environment or habitat. Dr. Vincent was the first person to study seahorses in the ocean, to identify threats to seahorses, and to start a seahorse conservation project. She is the Director of Project Seahorse, which she co-founded in 1996. This international organization works to help marine environments stay healthy and well-managed (not over-fished). Project Seahorse and its partners have helped seahorses by creating no-fishing zones and by promoting new laws.

Dr Vincent has a very interesting job. She is helping to save our seahorses and our seas! She's a hero to me. Imagine being the very first or the very best. I think that is so cool! Dr. Vincent is making a difference. I've met lots of kids who want to be marine biologists. Wouldn't you like to have an interesting job like Dr. Vincent? You can learn more about Dr. Vincent and Project Seahorse at **www.projectseahorse.org.**

How many seahorses can you see in this picture? (Hint, there are two).

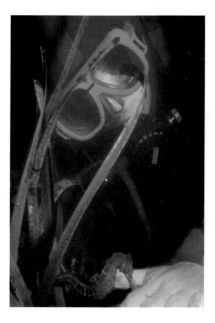

Here is Dr. Vincent at work under the sea. Nice office. Can you see the seahorse?

...and Become a Citizen Scientist

There are many ways that you and your family can volunteer to help our beaches to become better habitats for plants and animals. Here's an example.

In southern California, a group of volunteers helps scientists to monitor the spawning (egg-laying) activities of small fish called Grunions. Grunions are found only in California and Baja California, They come ashore to lay their eggs twice a month, at full moon and new moon high tides, from April to October. Thousands of fish might come ashore at one time. These eggs are an important food source for other animals. This project, called the Grunion Project, is not only helping to protect the grunions, it is teaching people to view our beaches as habitats. Volunteers are called "Grunion Greeters". Learn more about this project at: **www.grunion.org.**

These Grunion fish come ashore to lay their eggs! Scientists and volunteers of the Grunion Project are helping us to understand more about Grunions and more about our beaches as important habitats.

If you want to help scientists study plants or animals at the beach—or in your community—you can become a "citizen scientist". Citizen scientists are volunteers who observe nature and report their observations to a science project. Cornell Laboratory of Ornithology in New York is one of the largest citizen scientist sponsors in the U.S. If you like wild birds, you want to learn more about them, and you want to help scientists learn, you'll find lots of opportunities at the Cornell website. Visit it for more information: **www.cornell.birds.edu.**

Citizen Science programs are alive and well in Canada as well. Check out the Stewardship Canada Citizen Science website at **www.stewardshipcanada.ca.** On their home page, drop down the **Communities** menu and choose "Citizen Science."

Ocean Careers

There are lots of careers that focus on ocean ecology, too many to list in this space. But here are a few you might want to consider.

Marine Biologist
A person who studies plants, animals and other organisms that live in the ocean.

Oceanographer
A person who studies oceans. Oceanographers work in many areas. They might map the oceans, study the physics and chemistry of ocean waters, study marine biology, or study the way we use oceans' resources.

Keep one thing in mind; science is very important in these fields, so keep your science grades up. Of course, you'll also need to keep your math grades up and, heck, just keep working hard in all areas of school. Then you'll be able to choose whatever career you want to have!

Sand Experiments

To experience the constant movement of sand, stand in the ocean near the water's edge. Let the water run over your feet. The longer you stand, the further into the sand you'll sink. You're sinking because the water is washing the sand away from around and under your feet.

Congratulations! You're a Sea Star!

Congratulations! Here you are at the end of the book. Now that you've discovered nature at the beach, can you understand why I think it's such a cool place to explore? I hope you saw plants and animals that you never noticed before. There are so many others you might see that I couldn't possibly fit them all in this book, such as seals, sea lions, whales, raccoons, rabbits, mice, lizards, alligators, and a gazillion insects. Each time you take a beach walk you can see something different. Nature is always changing and there is so much more to the beach than building sand castles. Of course building sand castles is a lot of fun and having fun is pretty darn important.

I hope that as you learn more about nature and our environment, you'll find little ways in which you can make a difference to improve our planet. Just sharing this book with your friends and family can make a difference. Imagine if everyone in the world understood that beaches are more than just fun in the sun—they are important habitats. Now **that** would make a difference.

This seagull is holding a starfish. Wait a minute! There is no such animal as a seagull and no starfish, either. WOW! Things sure have changed since I was a kid! LOL

When you don't have the time for a long walk at the beach—or anywhere else—try taking my 20-Second Nature Break™. Twenty seconds is enough time to look around you to see which plants and animals are nearby. Try to take a nature break or a nature walk every day. It's good for your body, your mind, and your soul.

Thank you for taking this walk with me. Now it's your turn to share the wonderful discoveries and adventures you've had at the beach with your friends and family. After all, I shared, didn't I? Oh, and in case you've been wondering, yes, I had a name for my seahorse. His name was "Charlie". See you in the outdoors!

Have you read my other Take A Walk® Books?

takeawalk.com